Science on the Edge

CAVE SLEUTHS

LAURIE LINDOP

Twenty-First Century Books
Minneapolis

Dedicated to Blyth Hazen

Cover photograph courtesy of © Kevin Downey Photography
Photographs courtesy of Megan L. Porter: p. 4; © Kevin Downey Photography: pp. 10, 14, 20, 42,
43, 48, 51 (right), 62; © Jerry Horton: p. 13; © Stephen Alvarez/AURORA: p. 21; NPS Photo: p. 23
(© Peter Jones); www.VintageViews.org: p. 25; National Speleological Society, Inc.: p. 28 (© David
Jagnow); © Jim Pisarowicz: p. 31; © Peter Essick/AURORA: p. 34; © Kenneth Ingham: p. 36;
Woods Hole Oceanographic Institution: p. 39 (top: © R. Catanach); University of Delaware: p. 39
(bottom); © Dave Bunnell: pp. 44, 55; © Ephimia Morphew: p. 46; Visuals Unlimited: pp. 51 (left ©
Richard Thom), 52 (© Patrice Ceisel), 73 (© Albert Copley); © Tom Aley: p. 57; © Dr. David C.
Ashley: p. 57 (inset); © Dr. Thomas M. Iliffe: pp. 65, 68; © Annette Summers Engel: p. 72.
Illustrations by Ron Miller.

Twenty-First Century Books
A division of Lerner Publishing Group
241 First Avenue North
Minneapolis, Minnesota 55401 U.S.A.

Website address: www.lernerbooks.com

Library of Congress Cataloging-in-Publication Data

Lindop, Laurie.
Cave sleuths / Laurie Lindop.
p. cm. — (Science on the edge)
Summary: Discusses the science of speleology and what scientists have learned about caves, how
they are formed, and what lives in them.
Includes bibliographical references (p.   ).
ISBN-13: 978-0-7613-2702-8 (lib. bdg.)
ISBN-10: 0-7613-2702-9 (lib. bdg.)
1. Caves—Juvenile literature. 2. Speleology—Juvenile literature. [1. Speleology. 2. Caves.] I. Title.
GB601.2.L54   2006   551.44'7—dc22   2003016946

Manufactured in the United States of America
1 2 3 4 5 6 — DP — 11 10 09 08 07 06

CONTENTS

Engel collecting samples from the walls of Movile Cave

4

Introduction

In 1995, Annette Summers Engel, a geology graduate student from the University of Cincinnati, could hardly believe that she was halfway around the world and on her way to visit Movile Cave. Although young, Engel was one of only a handful of cave scientists in the world, and the Romanians wanted her to help them figure out Movile's age and how it had formed.

Almost a decade before, a group of construction workers in Romania had been doing exploratory digging for a nuclear power plant when they hit a strange void under the earth. It turned out they'd accidentally tapped into a cave system that had existed undisturbed for millions of years. Most remarkably, it was filled with thriving mats of bacteria and populations of never-before-seen animals, including blind spiders, snails, leeches, and scorpions.

Engel stared out the van's windows as the driver maneuvered through a trash dump in Romania. She knew that somewhere nearby was the artificial entrance shaft leading to the cave. When the van stopped beside a large cement platform covered with graffiti, Engel and four other researchers got out. Movile sure didn't look impressive from the surface! In the middle of the cement platform was a steel grate to keep vandals from climbing down the shaft and into the cave.

A flimsy wire ladder extended down to another platform about 10 feet (3 meters) below. The ladder's rungs were only one boot-length wide and were made of thin wire cable. Although she'd done a lot of caving in the United States, Engel had never climbed a ladder like this before. "There's a first time for everything," Engel told herself when it was her turn to descend.[1] She fit her caving helmet on over the bandanna holding back her hair and then hoisted her gear bag onto her back. Wrapping one leg around the side of the ladder, she held on tight with her hands and planted a boot on the first rung. The ladder swung and the wire pinched her skin as she made her slow descent. At the bottom, she snapped on her helmet's light. Here was an airtight plastic door as well as a brush that Engel used to wipe her caving coveralls and boots. She wanted to make sure she didn't track in surface soil, which could contaminate the cave's fragile environment.

On the other side of this air lock door she found herself inside a small rocky passage that was part of the Movile Cave system. Engel grinned. This was what she loved—squirming underground, seeing things most people could barely imagine. At 5 feet 4 inches (163 centimeters), she was just small enough to be able to sit upright and scoot down the passage, pushing her bag ahead of her with her boots. The walls left yellowish clumps—like tapioca grains—on her coveralls. These clumps, called ooids, were caused by water corroding the rock. Engel paused to scrape a few samples into a vial.

It was hot in the cave and as steamy as a sauna. A very smelly sauna. The rotten-egg stench came from a gas called hydrogen sulfide, which bubbled up into the cave with the water. As Engel continued scooting down the tunnel, she noticed that it was hard to breathe because the sealed cave had less oxygen than she was used to.

Up ahead, her headlamp shone on a rocky wall that looked like the passage's dead end. Actually, there was a narrow opening near the floor, nicknamed The Squeeze. Engel maneuvered around so that she was lying on her stomach. She pushed her bag through The Squeeze and then began wriggling through the tight slot. It felt like the rock was swallowing her. She pushed with her toes while pulling herself through with her hands.[2] On the other side, she was in a larger space with enough room to stand. Here the smooth walls looked like they'd been splashed with yellow, orange, and pink paint. When Engel tilted her head upward, her light shone on the cave's rounded ceiling, which looked rather like a cathedral's dome.

After crawling through a few more passages, Engel reached her destination, a murky gray lake covered with bubbly scum. All around the lake, the walls were covered with gypsum crystals, a mineral that looked like diamonds when Engel's light bounced off of it.

Engel opened up her bag and took out her field notebook. In it, she'd written down a list of scientific tasks she wanted to accomplish. She'd been warned that there was a chance the hydrogen sulfide in the air might cause her to lose her memory temporarily. She'd made this list just in case she started to feel woozy.[3]

First, she sterilized a pair of tweezers by dipping them in alcohol and using a lighter to burn away any contaminants. Then she began collecting soil, clay, and rock samples.

After a couple of hours, it was time to leave the toxic cave and head back toward fresh air. Before she did, she took a moment to sit quietly by the murky lake. Beyond the glow of her headlamp seeped the impenetrable darkness. She trained her lamp about the sparkling gypsum walls and saw creatures slowly emerge from hiding—blind spiders crept from nooks and crannies, and blind water insects darted across the pond's scum. All of them were unusual, living down here in a chemical world without light. Too soon, she stood to go. Unlike these insects, her body wasn't made to survive with so little oxygen and so much hydrogen sulfide.

CHAPTER ONE

A New Science

In today's world where nearly every inch of dry land has been mapped, where almost every mountain has been climbed and every ocean crossed, it may seem like there are few opportunities left for original exploration. But millions of caves twist beneath the surface of the Earth and only a small percentage have been investigated. For the true explorers, caves hold a powerful allure. "I have heard the drumming of my heart while surrounded by solid stone . . . as I struggle to move. . . ." wrote cave specialist Ronal Kerbo. "I have felt the pull of the darkness from the lip of a great open pit beneath the earth, and wondered just for a moment why there are people who will never take the first step—from which all great journeys begin."[1]

Until recently, few researchers were willing to take this step. Caving was an oddball hobby enjoyed by a few rugged individuals who didn't mind getting dirty while wriggling around underground. In general, these cavers were interested in pushing themselves to see how far they could go, and science was the last thing on their minds.

It wasn't until the late nineteenth century that a Parisian named Edouard-Alfred Martel developed a disciplined approach to exploring and mapping caves.

The entrance zone of Deer Cave in Borneo is more than 400 feet (122 meters) high.

The Father of Speleology

Many European caves can be reached only by dropping into deep black holes, known as pits, which then lead to cave systems. To determine a pit's depth, Martel had assistants tie a rope to a 6-pound (2.7-kilogram) cannonball and drop the cannonball over the edge. They'd measure how much rope it took for the cannonball to hit bottom, and then they'd rig a rope ladder of that same length. Martel would don coveralls and fill his pockets with six long candles. He'd strap a candle to his felt hat and begin climbing down.

Once inside a cave, Martel would take out a notebook and begin sketching a detailed map. He'd use a tape measure to calculate a chamber's size. To figure out vertical height, he'd attach a sponge to a balloon using a silk thread. Then he'd douse the sponge in alcohol and set it on fire. The heat would cause the balloon to rise to the cave ceiling. By measuring the balloon's string, he'd know the ceiling's height. As he traveled through the cave, he'd catalog everything he saw, including animals, interesting formations, and the course of underground streams.

In 1895, Martel founded a group dedicated to the exploration and scientific study of caves. He called this new field speleology (from the Greek words spelaion, meaning "cave," and logos, meaning "study"). Martel hoped that speleology would become a scientific discipline on a par with the more traditional fields such as biology or geology. For the most part, however, speleology remained as much sport as science.

It wasn't until the 1970s that scientists realized there was a lot more to these underground realms than meets the eye. At that time, they began to use the newly invented superpowerful electron microscope to look at samples taken from caves. "Just as the deep oceans became accessible to science only in the past few decades," said cave researcher Dr. Penny Boston, "now we're finding that kind of pioneering effort going on in caves."[2]

In this book, you will travel with a number of today's leading cave biologists, microbiologists, and geologists as they venture below the surface of the Earth into lightless worlds—some of which are as lovely as anything you can imagine, and some as dreadful.

The Devil's Pinch

Before heading underground, however, we need to learn a little bit about caving. There are two types of caving: horizontal and vertical. Horizontal caving involves walking and climbing through passages, and sometimes squeezing through tiny openings. Cavers give the worst squeezes names like The Agony, The Back Scratcher, The Claustrophobia Crawl, and The Grim Crawl of Death.

One of the most notorious squeezes, the Devil's Pinch, in the Bone-Norman Cave system in West Virginia, is a rocky slot that's about 20 feet (6 meters) long and ranges in height from 7 to 10 inches (18 to 25 centimeters). That means you have to slither on your belly through a long, dark slit so tiny that most rabbits would get stuck. Caver Michael Ray Taylor recalled that before attempting the Devil's Pinch, he took off his coveralls in order to gain that tiny extra clearance. He lay down on the ground and turned his head to the side. He started inching through the rock slit with one

Squeezing through the tiny passageway of the Devil's Pinch

arm ahead of him and the other dragging at his side. The rock dug into his bare chest and back. He pushed with his toes.

The tightest section was right at the end. Taylor asked his buddy on the other side to grab his arm. "Pull when I tell you to," Taylor ordered. He forced himself to relax. Exhaling, he said, "pull." His friend pulled. He moved forward a tiny bit, tried to inhale, but couldn't. The rock was squeezing him so tightly his lungs couldn't expand. "My arm felt as if Lee were yanking it out of its socket," he said. "I desperately dug both toes into the rock and pushed. . . . I slid forward an inch, and I could breathe again. My ribs were free of the Devil's Pinch."[3]

13

ending labyrinth, but rather contains approximately 2 miles (3.2 kilometers) of crisscrossed passageways. Caves like McDougal's are called "solution caves" because they are found in soluble, or dissolvable, rock, usually limestone that has been carved out by water over thousands, and sometimes even millions, of years. (Limestone is a rock composed mostly of a mineral known as calcite.)

There are about 17,000 known limestone caves in the United States, and they occur in every state except Louisiana and Rhode Island. The greatest concentration of caves can be found in the region where Tennessee, Alabama, and Georgia meet. Cavers have nicknamed this area TAG. Caves range dramatically in size from tiny crawlspaces to extensive underground systems.

The vast majority of caves around the world are found in a specific limestone terrain called karst. The name karst comes from the Kras region of Slovenia, an area with few surface rivers, patchy soil, and bare white limestone rock pocked with deep cave entrances. In karst regions, most water from rainfall and snowmelt rapidly seeps underground where it drains away through subterranean channels (caves).

A Cave Is Born

A solution cave begins to form when rainwater seeps down through the soil. As it does, the water picks up carbon dioxide from organic reactions and becomes slightly acidic. This acid, called carbonic acid, is the same stuff that gives soda pop its fizz. The acidic water makes its way down through cracks in the limestone bedrock.

THE FORMATION OF A LIMESTONE CAVE

Rainwater becomes slightly acidic as it seeps down through surface soil to the bedrock below. This weak acid is capable of dissolving rock, such as limestone.

Over hundreds of thousands of years, the acidic water will enlarge small cracks into larger cavities as the limestone is carried away in solution. If the water table lowers, some of these cavities, or caves, may be exposed to the air.

Caves

Mineral-bearing water seeping down from the surface creates stalactites, stalagmites, and other formations in the caves. A sinkhole might form if the surface soil collapses into the cavity in the underlying bedrock.

Sinkhole

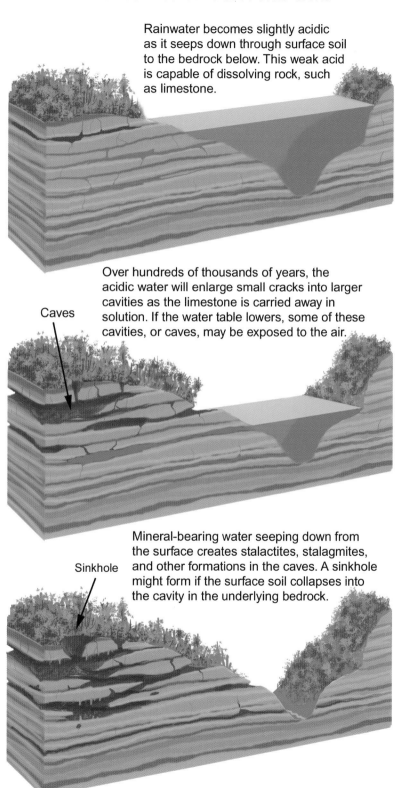

Gravity keeps pulling the water downward until it reaches a zone where all available pockets and cracks are filled with water. The top of this saturated zone is called the water table. (If you've ever looked down a well, the water table is at the level of the water.) At this point, the water spreads out sideways through cracks in the bedrock. As it does, the carbonic acid slowly eats away the limestone, forming channels.

Over time, some channels grow larger than others. This allows them to take in more water and, as a result, they grow larger still. Eventually certain channels will reach a critical size—about 0.2 inch (0.51 centimeter). At this point they become the dominant channels and take over most of the water in the area. Scientists aren't sure why 0.2 inch seems to be a benchmark size, but it may be because at this point, the water flow becomes more turbulent, drastically increasing its ability to dissolve and erode the surrounding limestone.

In some caves, like those in Bermuda, passages are carved out above the water table where freshwater and saltwater mix. In others, like Mammoth Cave in Kentucky, most of the passages form along the water table where flow rates are greatest, bringing maximum amounts of carbonic acid in contact with the surrounding limestone.

Some water-carved channels may become air-filled if the water table is lowered. This can happen if the climate becomes drier or if a nearby river carves out its bed, allowing the whole area's water table to migrate down deeper into the earth. Nearby cave cavities are suddenly above the water table and are filled with air. Over long periods of time, as the water level continues to drop, more and more passageways become air-filled and ready for exploration.

FORMATIONS INSIDE CAVES

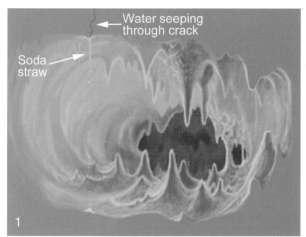

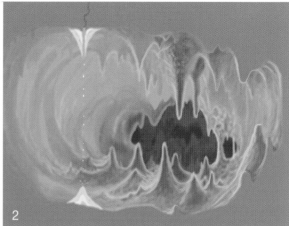

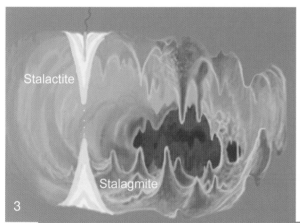

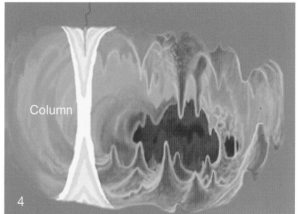

As rainwater flows down through the bedrock toward a cave passage, it gradually becomes saturated with dissolved limestone. When the water reaches an air-filled cavern, a chemical process causes the water to shed its limestone in the form of calcite crystals. In places where there is a steady drip, the calcite may build a hollow tube called a soda straw (1). If the inside of the straw becomes blocked, the water will start to flow down the outside (2). Eventually a hornlike shape forms. This is called a stalactite. Water that drips incessantly onto the floor of a cave will build up a similar formation, called a stalagmite (3). If a stalactite and a stalagmite grow and meet, they form a column (4).

A cave room full of
unusually long soda straws

Depending on how water drips into a cave, other types of formations develop. These are given vivid names like fried eggs, draperies, cave pearls, and popcorn. This "cave flower" was found in Mammoth Cave, Kentucky.

CHAPTER THREE

Mystery at Carlsbad Caverns

"Darnedest things I ever saw," muttered geology student Harvey DuChene back in 1971.[1] He was on a trip through Carlsbad Caverns, New Mexico, with three other young geology students, including Carol Hill. In one of the cave's large rooms, the group paused to rest. As they sat in a circle, they discussed the many mysteries surrounding them. Nothing in their geology textbooks could begin to explain Carlsbad's unique features.

This trip would eventually inspire Carol Hill to pursue a period of intensive research that would "change the course of

This stunning room in Carlsbad Caverns is named the Doll's Theater.

speleology, and would also help bring it into the position of a 'respectable' science, rather than an amateur effort by a 'bunch of grubby cavers.'"[2]

Not Just Any Old Hole in the Ground

Carlsbad Caverns is a cave system of three hundred known caves that twist deep beneath the sun-blasted Guadalupe Mountains. If you were to drive out to these mountains and stare at the cacti and parched earth, you might find it hard to believe that 250 million years ago the area was part of a shallow inland sea. Here, a spectacular living barrier reef stretched across what is now the desert of west Texas and New Mexico. The reef was made up of millions of organisms that secrete calcite. Combined with saltwater and aided by encrusting organisms, the calcite cemented into limestone. Over time, the water grew too salty and became toxic to the reef-building organisms. Eventually the reef ceased to grow and the basin was covered under hundreds of feet of sediment.

Carlsbad's extensive cave system was discovered in 1898 by Jim White, a young cowhand. White was on his way home for supper at the Triple X Ranch when he froze in his tracks. A black cloud was rising straight out of the dusty ground. As White said later, "I thought it was a volcano, but then I'd never seen a volcano."[3] Moving closer, he realized it was a swarm of bats exiting from a hole in the ground. Curious, he waited until the last bat flew away and then lit a dead cactus and dropped it down the hole. It fell about 200 feet (61 meters) before splattering. After this, White was obsessed with the cave—at every opportunity, he'd fire up a kerosene lantern and climb down a ladder to explore new regions. It seemed to him that there was no end to its wonders. He wrote:

> Suspended from the ceilings were mammoth chandelier-clusters of stalactites in every size and color. Walls that were frozen cascades of glittering flowstone, jutting rocks that held suspended long, slender formations that rang when I touched them—like a key on the xylophone. . . . I encountered hundreds of pools filled with pure water as clear as glass.[4]

A local merchant heard Jim White's account of the cave in 1901, and while the merchant had no interest in the cave's beauty, he realized that farmers were willing to pay good money for bat dung (called guano), which they used as fertilizer. The merchant applied for a mining claim and then drilled a shaft into the cave's bat chamber. He built a contraption that would lower a big bucket into the cave to carry the guano to the surface.

By the early 1920s the bat guano had been depleted and mining stopped. The cave was turned over to the U.S. government, and Jim White started a tiny tourist business, lowering visitors down into the cave via the rickety guano bucket. Eventually word of Carlsbad's wonders spread to Wash-

Jim White stands with the old bucket that he used to lower the first tourists into Carlsbad Caverns.

ington, D.C. The government dispatched a mineral expert to determine whether the cave should be deemed a national monument. "I am wholly conscious of the feebleness of my efforts to convey in words the deep conflicting emotions," the expert enthused in his report, "the feeling of fear and awe . . . [at] such a complex [grouping] of natural wonders."[5] In 1923, Carlsbad Caverns was officially proclaimed a national monument, and seven years later, it became a national park.

A half century later, the park was a leading tourist attraction with about 500,000 visitors traveling through it annually. The section open to the public had electric lights and paved trails. A park sign explained that Carlsbad Caverns had been formed 3 to 4 million years ago when rainwater carrying carbonic acid seeped down to the limestone and slowly ate away all the rock. It turned out that the sign was wrong.

Sleuthing for Clues

In 1971, Carol Hill sat in Carlsbad's Mystery Room staring at the walls, which were so soft she could push in her finger ¼ to ¾ of an inch (0.6 to 1.9 centimeters). She thought about the house-sized blocks of gypsum she'd encountered, which were really unusual because gypsum normally dissolves easily. If water carved the cave, the gypsum should have been flushed away long ago. What really puzzled her was the size of some of the caverns. "The Big Room in Carlsbad Cavern is the biggest cave room in North America," she said. "That's a lot of limestone to be carried away."[6]

She'd seen Mammoth Cave, a typical solution cave, where "you can follow the path of the water from beginning to end just like some kind of elaborate plumbing system. But you can't do that for Carlsbad. The cave keeps stopping where it shouldn't."[7]

Her curiosity aroused, Hill was determined to try to solve Carlsbad's mysteries. She decided the first step was to figure out where all that gypsum had come from. She knew that if she added drops of sulfuric acid to a limestone chunk, the stone dissolved away in a fizz, leaving behind powdery gypsum. If sulfuric acid had been present in Carlsbad, it might have carved out the complex cave system. "But," as her colleague Dave Jagnow pointed out, "you very rarely find [sulfuric acid] in nature."[8]

Carol Hill traveled the parched landscape around the Guadalupe Mountains looking for a source of sulfuric acid. The answer turned out to be more obvious than she'd expected. Oil rigs dotted the flatlands, and she found out that the oil pumped up by them was tainted with hydrogen sulfide. As Jagnow later explained, "Any time you drill a well around the Guadalupe Mountains you smell this rotten egg smell—hydrogen sulfide gas."[9] Most important, when hydrogen sulfide comes in contact with oxygen, it produces sulfuric acid.

Carol Hill concluded that at Carlsbad, hydrogen sulfide–laced water bubbling from deep inside the Earth must have mixed with oxygen in the air and in rainwater to create a lot of acid. This acid, stronger than carbonic acid, dissolved the limestone bedrock, leaving behind gypsum. As it did, it produced carbon dioxide as a byproduct. This carbon dioxide, when combined with water, formed carbonic acid. In combination, these two acids would be capable of dissolving immense amounts of limestone.

Scientist Carol Hill examines some of the oddities in Carlsbad Caverns.

"This," Carol Hill admitted, "was a totally new idea," and many fellow geologists were skeptical. "They thought all caves were formed by underground rivers. . . . The old-timers had no concept of acid coming up from below."[10] In their defense, she added, "Carlsbad and the other caves in the Guadalupe Mountains are formed differently than most other caves in the world."[11]

It wasn't until the 1990s that Hill's theory was fully accepted by academics. The final proof came when a handful of active sulfuric acid caves, like Romania's Movile Cave, were discovered, where skeptics could see for themselves how the acid ate away at the limestone. One of these sulfuric acid caves, located in the Mexican rain forest, could be in your worst nightmares, although for cave scientists, it has turned out to be a dream come true.

CHAPTER FOUR

The Creepy Cave

In 1987 cavers Jim Pisarowicz and Warren Netherton traveled to the state of Tabasco in southern Mexico because they wanted to find new caves to explore. Part of the Tabasco region is karst and gets lots of rain, which means lots of caves.

Pisarowicz knew the best way to find these caves was by asking the locals. When he queried people in the sleepy village of Tapijulapa, they held their noses and told him to follow a trail to a white stream that would lead him to a cave called Cueva de

Villa Luz (Cave of the Lighted House). As he and Netherton splashed along the banks of the white stream, they soon noted the rotten-egg stench of sulfur. The stench kept getting stronger, and soon they found the cave entrance. After walking down a stone staircase built by the locals, Pisarowicz entered the cave and stared about in awe.

In twenty years of caving he'd never seen anything like this. Rubbery gray stalactites hung from the ceiling, looking so much like mucus he dubbed them "snottites." As he waded in a little deeper, schools of pale pink fish swam around his boots. Everywhere he looked, he saw gypsum. Its crystals caught the glow of his headlamp and sparkled orange and yellow. In other places, the walls were covered with gooey white gypsum paste that made him think of melting cake icing.

The weird snottites that scientists found in Cueva de Villa Luz in Mexico

The acid dripping onto him from the snottites and cave walls was dissolving his clothing and burning his skin. His lungs ached from the foul hydrogen sulfide gas, and he beat a hasty retreat knowing that too much exposure to this gas can bring about memory loss and even death. Clearly this cave was in the midst of being formed by sulfuric acid in exactly the way that Carol Hill had hypothesized it had happened long ago at Carlsbad Caverns.

Pisarowicz returned to Villa Luz a year later with a group of cavers to conduct a thorough survey, but found he couldn't keep them inside the cave. "This is the first time I had ever been in a cave where the survey crew mutinied because they were being burned by acid," he reported.[1] Anywhere acid touched, it ate right through clothes and flesh. It pitted headlamps and turned leather boots to mush. As one caver reported, "You don't want to get too close [to the acidic walls] because you feel they'll digest you."[2]

Pisarowicz was determined to locate scientists who'd be willing to put up with the dangers to study this bizarre cave. It took until 1996 for him to find a willing scientist. Geologist Louise Hose was a former cycling champion and loved adventure. "As soon as we got into the cave's first room, I knew this was the beginning of something big," she recalled. "I just didn't know how big."[3] They collected slime and snottite samples and brought them back to the United States. In a lab run by a fellow caver named Norman Pace, they used a powerful electron microscope to scan their samples. They made a startling discovery: The samples were alive! Millions of never-before-seen microbes (microscopic organisms) made up the cave's strange formations.

Right away they set about arranging a new expedition for January 1998, and this time they didn't have trouble attracting scientists from numerous disciplines. To protect them from the hydrogen sulfide, they'd wear gas masks. Unfortunately, however, those masks wouldn't help filter out other potentially deadly gases in the cave, including carbon monoxide. As one of Villa Luz's visitors put it, in places, "The carbon monoxide levels rev so high it's equivalent to running a NASCAR race in a tool shed."[4]

As Gross As It Gets

At the smelly entrance to Villa Luz, the scientists put on their cumbersome rubber gas masks. Team member Kenneth Ingham checked the electronic gas monitor, which would beep like crazy if they encountered any potentially deadly spikes—something that everyone knew was entirely likely.

The team penetrated 1 mile (1.6 kilometers) into the cave, mapping a number of unexplored areas. They came upon skylights where the cave roof had collapsed and fresh air circulated through the toxic environment. Sometimes they'd see a poor surface creature that had fallen into Villa Luz and died.

As they traveled, the team paused now and then to collect water samples from the milky stream twisting through the cave. They took readings of the air quality and discovered that the hydrogen sulfide levels ranged from nearly 0 to 125 parts per million (the U.S. government considers 10 ppm to be the maximum tolerance level for working without full protective and breathing gear). They noted a variety of creatures living in this foul environment. Seven species of bats, including vampire bats, hung upside down, and beneath them, their guano crawled with maggots and insects. Clouds of midges, or small flies, hovered

Biologist Penny Boston (in the green hat) and other team members, including Diana Northup, collect samples from a stream in Cueva Luz.

around the dripping snottites. Spiders, including black widows, covered whole sections of walls with a startling density. In the river darted eels, albino crabs, and schools of fish.

In one cramped section of the cave, Dr. Penny Boston squatted beside a wall covered in snottites. From her pack, she took out a vial filled with a special chemical called fixative to preserve specimens. Dr. Boston held the bottle under the snottite while Dr. Diana Northup used sterile tweezers to clip it from the ceiling. Dr. Boston recalled:

The snottite slips from Diana's instrument. . . . My foot, protected by an army boot, slips in the slimy, acid-soaked

34

gypsum paste that could easily burn through my skin. . . . Our [gas] masks seem to bore into our skulls and faces. We long to get out of this choking place and breathe the sweet air of the surface. Finally, the sample slides into the sterile tube. Capture! We have the best! As we pack our gear . . . Kenneth Ingham . . . gives the word that the carbon monoxide level is rising and we leave immediately. Our masks provide no protection against that deadly gas. . . . We try to hurry . . . We slip and the sharp rocks slice into our skin . . . My skull is working on a weird headache that seems as if my brain is growing larger and my eyes are sinking in, but I am oddly detached from the feeling. The pain . . . tells me we've been in too long. I've picked up a toxic load of hydrogen sulfide through my skin, and perhaps a touch of carbon monoxide poisoning as well.[5]

Webs of Life

The scientists wondered how a cave like Villa Luz, so deadly to humans, could support such an energetic ecosystem. Everywhere they looked life buzzed, dripped, flew, and swarmed around them. "Usually when you walk into a cave, life is something that you have to look pretty hard to see," said Diana Northup, "and something that just strikes you, just slaps you in the face at Villa Luz is the fact that everywhere you look, there's life—there's spiders, there's insects, and as you go deeper into the cave and into the dark areas, there are rocks in the stream that are covered with this green [mosslike] coating. It's not being driven by sunlight. It has to be driven by other things."[6]

CHAPTER FIVE

Extremophiles

The first extremophiles were discovered in 1977 when the research submarine Alvin dove down a record 1.6 miles (2.6 kilometers) to investigate a region where the deep-sea floor was spreading apart. The submarine drifted over miles of desolation before its spotlight lit up an oasis—clams, mussels, and weird giant tube worms clustered around shimmering clouds of hot water and minerals spewing out of vents from deep inside the Earth. Scientists discovered that microbes derived energy from this chemical stew. In turn, they served as a food source for the larger creatures.

The research submarine *Alvin* transmitted the first images of extremophiles, which were found living in seemingly inhospitable conditions at the bottom of the sea.

Scientists were astounded to find these giant red worms living inside white tubes near vents on the ocean floor.

Most scientists assumed that the deep-sea microbes were related to surface organisms that had migrated downward and evolved to survive in complete darkness. Scientist Thomas Gold, on the other hand, proposed that the microbes rose up from inside the Earth, from a region once thought too extreme for any life to exist. He suggested that there was a small dead zone beneath the Earth's soil and the ocean floor, but that if scientists looked deeper than this, they'd find vast colonies of microbes living in a deep, hot biosphere—deep because it could extend 6.2 miles (10 kilometers) or more beneath the surface, and hot because temperatures would approach or exceed 212°F (100°C).

To test his theory, Gold conducted a deep-drilling test. He found microbes living more than 3 miles (4.8 kilometers) down near ancient petroleum deposits. Although his team carefully sterilized their equipment, skeptics contended that the microbes were actually from the surface and had been on the drill itself when it went into the ground.

Into a Man-Made Cave

In the mid-1990s geomicrobiologist Tullis Onstott realized there were other ways to descend far underground. He traveled to South Africa to some of the deepest gold mines in the world. He dropped into these man-made caves via a steel cage elevator. At 1.9 miles (3 kilometers) below the Earth's surface, the temperature of the rock rose to 140°F (60°C). With his shirt drenched in sweat from the 100 percent humidity, Onstott crawled down the miners' tunnels. "The footing is bad; it's noisy; you can't see; there's dust all over the place; and the noise of the [miners'] air hammers is incredible," said one of his colleagues.[1]

Onstott took a hammer to a section of newly blasted wall and knocked loose a chunk of uncontaminated rock. Here, deep inside the Earth, he found extremophile microbes that consumed chemicals in the rock and reproduced only once every few hundred thousand or even a million years.

As Dr. Penny Boston said, "We have begun to realize that wherever we seem to look, wherever there are energy sources for them to live on, we actually find life forms. And maybe they're not really obvious, and maybe you have to look really hard, but they exist."[2]

Because they exist in extreme environments, extremophiles tend to be very hard for scientists to collect. You either have to dig very far down, find ways to protect yourself from boiling temperatures, travel into the Arctic deep freeze, or you can snap on a headlight and go into a cave. While caving's not particularly easy, to some scientists it beats making a trek to the South Pole! By the mid-1990s cave scientists were making big news with their discoveries of cave extremophiles.

A Tasty Meal of Rocks

It is hard to imagine a more extreme environment than Lechuguilla (lay-chew-GEE-ya) Cave. Part of the Guadalupe Mountains cave system in Texas and New Mexico, Lechuguilla, or Lech as cavers call it, was originally assumed to extend no farther than its 90-foot (27-meter) entrance pit. In 1986, however, a group of intrepid cavers dug through many feet of rubble to be met by a blast of air from what turned out to be the deepest limestone cave in the United States. It's also one of the toughest to explore. Writer Jon Krakauer described a trip into Lechuguilla:

Scientists found Lechuguilla to be one of the most difficult caves to explore—a place of pitch-blackness, total silence, and many hazards.

We slithered like lizards down narrow slots . . . and dangled tenuously above yawning chasms. . . . Although fraught with hazards, Lechuguilla is a place of phantasmal beauty. Cramped, twisting passages open suddenly into spaces as cavernous as Madison Square Garden, the walls sparkling with brilliant white crystals. Opalescent cave "pearls" lie in clusters at the bottom of shallow pools.[3]

In 1989, Kiym Cunningham, a U.S. Geological Survey scientist, used an electron microscope to look at some rock samples

These fantastic gypsum crystals in Lechuguilla are found in a room named the Chandelier Ballroom. Until these were discovered in Lech, scientists thought gypsum crystals could grow only about 6 feet (1.8 meters) long.

Lake Castrovalva is considered to be one of the most beautiful areas in Lech. Scientists must swim down a 150-foot (46-meter) waterway to reach this lake.

from Lech. He discovered filaments that might be fossilized life. This intriguing find inspired Diana Northup to begin conducting microbial studies at Lech. She tracked down a few extremophile bugs unique to Lech and was soon joined by microbiologist Larry Mallory and biologist Penny Boston.

Inside Lech, the scientists placed microscope slides on rocks covered with a brown mudlike material they'd nicknamed "gorilla poop" to see what, if anything, would grow on them. They scratched the rock with sterilized loops of wire and then rubbed those wires over a specially prepared gel in petri dishes. They used sterile syringes to extract droplets from the cave's pools, which were so clear that the water wasn't visible.

The diversity stunned them—thousands of never-before-seen species were living in complex ecosystems. As Dr. Larry Mallory put it, "If I wanted to collect a redwood tree, a tiger, and a trout, I'd be collecting much more closely related organisms than many that live in a single water droplet . . . in Lechuguilla."[4]

These microbes were able to derive energy from the traces of manganese, iron, and sulfur found in the rocks themselves. The discovery of rock-eating microbes drew more researchers to Lech, including teams of NASA scientists who thought that there might be an important link between the cave and the planet Mars.

Searching for Life in Caves on Mars

Today, Mars is a freezing cold, barren desert without any visible signs of life, but 4 billion years ago, Earth and Mars had very similar climates. Scientists have long theorized that life might have developed on the Red Planet, just like it did here on Earth, but as conditions worsened on Mars, all life there was extinguished. With the discovery of mineral-loving microbes living in Lech's barren tunnels, scientists began to wonder if similar microbes might still exist beneath the Martian surface. "Organisms would be shielded from intense ultraviolet radiation there. . . ." said NASA's Chris McKay. "In the absence of sunlight and organic matter, any . . . life would have to derive its energy entirely from mineral sources."[5]

Newspapers and magazines around the country ran the story with headlines like, "The Cave That Holds Clues to Life on Mars!" Lech's scientists were quick to point out that everything at this point was speculation. It would be one tough assignment to actually find a Martian cave and collect samples. After all, a round-trip would require between six hundred and one thousand days of travel. Further, caving on Mars would be even tougher than caving on Earth. Caving astronauts would have to wear space suits and air tanks that would seriously hamper their ability to maneuver through narrow spaces. There's also less gravity, so instead of walking normally, they would be bouncing along and bumping into rocks.

If scientists ever succeed in bringing back living Martian cave microbes, they will have to be very careful to keep them contained in the laboratory to ensure that they can't infect our planet. The horrors of such plagues have been fodder for science-fiction movies such as Outbreak and The Andromeda Strain. On the other hand, cave scientists say that if Martian cave microbes are anything like Earth's cave microbes, then they're just as likely to help humanity as hurt it.

In June 2002, Dr. Penny Boston and a group of NASA scientists simulated a Mars expedition in the Utah desert, complete with a stainless steel spaceship and space suits. Here, Boston is practicing extracting a "fossil" from surface rocks.

Dab On a Little Moonmilk
and Call Me in the Morning

In the sixteenth and seventeenth centuries, European doctors used to sprinkle moonmilk, a white, claylike substance found on cave walls, onto wounds. They didn't know why, but it helped patients heal. Scientists now know that moonmilk is made up of extremophile microbes. Because these microbes live in a low-nutrient cave environment, they produce powerful toxins to fight off other microbes that might challenge them for food. Sometimes, as in the case of moonmilk, these toxins can act like antibiotics, killing infections in humans.

In 1994 moonmilk wasn't on microbiologist Larry Mallory's mind when he wandered through Lechuguilla with Jason Richards, a cave specialist with the National Park Service. Mallory recalled that he was in the midst of taking microbial samples when Richards asked him what the microbes might be good for. "I said, 'Who knows?' I didn't know there was a reason to think they were good for anything. [Richards] said, 'Well, maybe they cure cancer?' I said, 'Well, they might.'"[6]

A few days later, Dr. Mallory got a call from Miles Hacker, a pharmacology researcher who was interested in seeing some of the Lech samples. Mallory sent him a variety of microbes, and a few days later, Hacker called him back. "This is the most exciting thing I've seen in fifteen years of drug research," Hacker told him.[7] The cave microbes were viciously attacking breast cancer cells like nothing Hacker had ever seen before. Soon Mallory and Hacker formed a company that would research the disease-fighting properties of various cave microbes.

47

Dr. Larry Mallory has done his most important work while back at his lab, where he started studying Lechuguilla microbes and helped begin the study of cave microbes as sources to fight cancer.

"You have to isolate a chemically pure bacterial product," explained Mallory, "figure out how it works, what else it kills, how it moves in the body, how long it remains effective, how much of it you need. These steps are all part of the long road of drug development. You want to kill the cancer but not the patient. The nice thing about developing a drug from bacteria is you don't worry about depleting a species. All you need is one."[8]

CHAPTER SIX

Bears and Bats and Troglobites, Oh My!

To thrive, all animals must live in suitable environments. Cave animals are no different—there are parts of a cave some animals prefer and other parts they don't. The biologists who study cave life, called speleobiologists, classify cave creatures based on how much time they spend in caves and which regions of a cave they choose to inhabit.

A lot of surface creatures will venture a short distance into caves looking for protection, to reproduce, or to hunt for food. Bears use caves for their long winter naps. Humans have used caves for shelter and, in some cases, spiritual reasons. Skunks, raccoons, and snakes will go into caves hoping to find dinner.

Animals that use caves on occasion, but do not live their entire lives in them, are called trogloxenes from the Greek words troglos ("cave") and xenos ("guest"). Some of the most well-known trogloxenes are bats.

Living in the Dark Zone

The section of a cave where there is no light is known as the dark zone. Here, the darkness is not like that of a moonless night. In the dark zone, the darkness is absolute. If you were to shut off your headlamp and lift your hand to your face, you would not be able to see even its outline.

Cave biologists divide the animals that live in this region into two groups. One group is the troglophiles, from troglos ("cave") and phileo ("love"). These creatures—like earthworms, salamanders, and beetles—are equally successful living in a cave's pitch-blackness as they are living in dark environments on the Earth's surface. Other creatures, known as troglobites, from troglos ("cave") and bios ("life"), spend their entire lives in the dark zones of caves.

Scientists believe that some of these troglobite species may have been surface dwellers that headed underground thousands of years ago in order to avoid extinction due to devastating climate changes. "Only such massive changes could account for the migration," said Valerio Sbordoni, a leading cave biologist. "The change probably occurred towards the end of the last Ice Age, when glaciers retreated from vast areas of the Earth and temperatures began to vary."[1]

Over time, the animals evolved to adapt to their pitch-black environment. Troglobites tend to have slow metabolisms, allow-

A colorless cave crayfish

The proteus cave salamander is one of the rarest troglobites.

ing them to survive on less food. Many lack eyes, which require energy to maintain. Some have long, spindly legs that they use to feel their way around and sensitive receptors under their skin for avoiding obstacles and detecting the presence of other creatures.

One thing that perplexed speleobiologists was why so many of these cave animals evolved to be pale. Of course there's no reason for them to have pigmentation (colors) if they can't see each other. On the other hand, it doesn't take any extra energy to maintain bright stripes, flecks, or polka dots. Pigmentation for cave dwellers is what scientists call a "neutral" trait.

Intrigued by this puzzle, evolutionary biologist Richard Borowsky embarked on a study in 1993 of the Mexican cave tetra, a fish related to the toothy piranha that lives in surface rivers. Dr. Borowsky makes it clear that he's not a caver by choice, but rather a scientist who goes into caves in search of creatures that will aid in all his research. "It takes lots of time and energy to find new caves and there's very little chance of [scientific] reward. I depend on the thousands of cavers who map caves and [who report sightings of potentially interesting cave fish]."[2]

Back at his lab, Dr. Borowsky transfers the Mexican cave tetras into aquariums. To study their genes, he anesthetizes the fish and then snips off small fin samples before returning the fish to their tanks. He extracts the genetic information using basic molecular biology techniques.

At one Mexican cave, Caballo Moro, Dr. Borowsky tracked down schools of eyeless tetras living in the dark zone. In another region of Caballo Moro, the cave roof had collapsed, allowing sunlight to filter down to the stream. Here, Dr. Borowsky found tetras with eyes. He thinks that the eyed fish are probably descendants of blind cave fish that reacquired eyes when there was a good reason to have them.

He found that the two types of cave tetras could be bred with each other as well as with their flashy, fully sighted surface relatives. By studying the offspring of these fish, Dr. Borowsky was able to identify some of the genes responsible for the cave-related traits. It turns out that the genes affecting pigment loss were linked to genes affecting metabolism. This showed that a neutral trait like pigment loss could be linked to a valuable trait like having a slow metabolism. No wonder so many troglobites lack pigment!

Further, the cave-related traits were all caused by multiple genes. For example, eye loss was caused by at least three different genes. This was an important discovery because many traits in the human population, including those responsible for some chronic diseases such as diabetes and hypertension, are thought to be caused by multiple genes. These multiple gene systems are little understood and difficult to study. Cave tetras make great research subjects.

"One beauty [of the Mexican cave fish]," Dr. Borowsky explained, "is that there are thirty different populations in caves ranging over a large 81 mile [130 kilometer] range."[3] These populations evolved independently to lose their eyes and they did so in different ways. Dr. Borowsky is currently figuring out which genes changed in populations A, B, and C—from Pachon, Molino, and Curva Caves—in order to determine if certain types of structural eye change are favored over others. By identifying the genes that go "bad" in cave fish and cause them to lose their eyes, he may learn about genes that cause similar changes in the eyes of humans suffering from conditions like age-related macular degeneration, which can lead to blindness.

Dr. Borowosky continues to regularly collect fish from Mexico and bring them back to his New York lab for further study. To transport them, he puts the fish in plastic bags much like you'd get at a fair. The fish have such slow metabolisms that they can last months without eating, so he doesn't have to worry about feeding them. Dr. Borowosky thinks this fact may hold clues to human obesity. While many factors can lead people to become overweight, a slow metabolism can cause people to put on more weight with less food. "As an evolutionist," Dr. Borowsky said, "I think it is fun to learn about these things, but there's also some practical use."[4]

CHAPTER SEVEN

Nature's Storm Drains

Caves act like nature's storm drains. When it rains, water can soak in from the ground or pour through a cave's opening(s). Cave geologist Louise Hose explained, "When it rains, a big surge of water can suddenly gush through a cave. You never know when it might happen, because in a deep cave you're unaware of the weather outside."[1]

When it rains, pollution from the surface can also easily flow into a cave. For example, in 1996 cave hydrologists (water experts) found that a seemingly pristine pool in Carlsbad Caverns was actually contaminated by runoff from an aboveground parking lot. During rainstorms, oil and brake fluids from the parking

Rain can present serious dangers to scientists who might be working inside a cave. Water can quickly fill passages, making it difficult to maneuver through the corridors.

lot drained off into the soil above the cave. Eventually the polluted water worked its way through the soil and rock to drip into the cave pools.

When pollutants enter caves, whole populations of creatures, including microbes, can be killed. It's hard to know how many never-before-seen creatures have disappeared from our planet due to surface pollution. In Yugoslavia, industrial pollution annihilated more than one hundred species of animals from a single underground river!

Recently, cave scientists have realized that because many troglobites are so sensitive to pollution, they can help alert us to contamination we might have otherwise overlooked. For example, meet the Tumbling Creek Cave snail.

My Love, My Cave Snail

The Tumbling Creek Cave snail is a troglobite that eats bacteria slime, lives under rocks, and is extremely lucky to be in the care of one of the world's leading cave hydrologists, Tom Aley. This bearded hulk of a man doesn't try to hide that he's in love with his cave snails. In fact, he's more than in love; he's obsessed with protecting a troglobite that's blind, translucent, and about as big as a grain of sand.

When Aley first bought the land that Tumbling Creek Cave is on, back in the 1970s, he counted about 15,000 cave snails. By 2001 the population had so decreased that he could find only 40 snails huddling upstream. What happened? Aley caught himself wishing he could "talk to the little specks, ask what was causing the problem, ask what he could do to fix it. [But] grain-sized translucent blind snails aren't big on conversation."[2]

The Tumbling Creek Cave snail is just one example of a species threatened by outside contaminants that have seeped into its cave.

Tom Aley injects dye into a stream from a tanker truck. This allows him to determine how much runoff travels from the surface area into the cave's streambed.

Aley guessed the problem had to do with contaminants seeping into his cave's stream. To find out, he conducted the following test: First, he dyed batches of moss in different colors—red, green, and peach—and injected them into streams surrounding the cave. Snapping on his headlamp, he then headed underground and deposited mesh bags filled with charcoal in the cave's streambed. Later, he collected the bags and analyzed them to see how many moss spores they'd collected and which colors had made their way into the cave.

From this test, he determined that a good deal of runoff traveled from the overgrazed farm above the cave through 100 feet (30 meters) of bedrock and straight into the stream, causing the water to turn murky with sediments. He sympathized with his snails' perspective: "You get covered in sediment, your food's covered in sediment, your gills are clogged with the sediment."[3]

If he was going to save the little specks, he'd have to rehabilitate the surrounding land. The previous owner, he said, "had about 500 cows on 1,350 acres [546 hectares]. When he cleared this pasture, he pushed all the trees into the valleys, where the stream has to cut around them and make more channels. We pull out the stumps and push the soil back where it belongs, make U-shaped swales and mulch them."[4] This work was costly, but Aley felt it was worth it because he was not only returning the land to its natural state, but he was saving his white flecks.

In 2001, Aley succeeded in getting his snails added to the U.S. Fish and Wildlife Service's list of endangered species. As one spokesman from the service explained: "The plight of the Tumbling Creek Cave snail is, unfortunately, typical of many cave species. They are seldom seen and often forgotten. But they can be barometers of the health of our natural systems, especially when we understand their dependence on clean water, something that is vital to all life."[5]

Spring Water—So Clear, So Clean?

Today, 50 percent of the United States relies on groundwater for its drinking water source. Groundwater is defined as all the water that's below the Earth's surface, including water in caves, between sand grains, and in cracks in the bedrock. In regions where the groundwater filters slowly through dense layers of sand and soil, many contaminants will be removed from the water. In karst regions, however, the water is able to move swiftly through the Swiss cheeselike holes in the bedrock and many toxins remain intact.

Tom Aley has been at the forefront of studying how groundwater moves through caves and how the path it takes can ultimately affect the purity of the water that comes out of our taps. "My first big successful [dye] trace was . . . in 1969," he recalled. He injected organic dye in a creek and then tracked its movement until it reemerged 18 miles (29 kilometers) away. "It was the longest trace ever done at that time, and it got a lot of attention in the press; it was even in The New York Times Sunday paper. According to the literature, I should have used hundreds of pounds of dye. I did it with 10 pounds [4.5 kilograms]."[6] He explained to reporters that the reason he needed so little dye was that the water had traveled through a cave system.

Aley made more headlines when he did a dye trace at Dora sinkhole, near Hodgson Mill, Missouri. A sinkhole is where a cave roof has collapsed. Water that flows into a sinkhole can't escape except by running through the cave. In the United States, sinkholes can range in size from shallow depressions to steep chasm openings that seem to disappear into infinite darkness. For generations, people have dumped trash into many of the deepest sinkholes, mistakenly assuming it would disappear deep into the Earth. In fact, the trash that gets dumped into sinkholes just sits there in that section of a cave. It will contaminate any groundwater that might flow around it.

At the Dora sinkhole, Aley carefully picked his way down the clifflike sides and found a huge pile of garbage, including aluminum cans, oil cans, and a dead pig. He also encountered some sort of black goopy stuff with a hardened crust that he couldn't identify. "I did a 'scientific study,' " he said. "I kicked it with my boot toe, found nothing, so then I climbed on top and stomped it with my heel. Again nothing. Then I found a fresher pile. This time when I stomped, the crust broke through and my leg went into it deep."[7] Aley had discovered the contents of a septic system cleaning truck.

He ran a dye trace on the Dora sinkhole and found that water ran from that sinkhole, through a cave system, and then came to the surface at a spring 15.5 miles (25 kilometers) away. This spring wasn't far from a well-known drinking hole where people would stop and sip what they thought was the freshest springwater on Earth. "After the story about the trace," Aley said, "the dumping in the sinkhole ended; it just ended. This said to me, people really do care, but they need the right information."[8]

CHAPTER EIGHT

Cave Diving

The hot Caribbean sun beat down on the scuba diving equipment tossed into the back of the pickup truck. Dr. Thomas Iliffe, known by many as the "father of cave diving for science," was wedged between the driver and his colleague, Brian Kakuk, head of the Bahama Caves Research Foundation. On March 18, 2000, they were on their way to investigate the creatures living in a water-filled cave that Kakuk had learned about. The cave was in the middle of Exuma Island's dense jungle. As they bounced along the rutted road in sweltering humidity, Dr. Iliffe looked forward to slipping into

One scientist has described the cave-diving experience this way: "The cave moves like a roller coaster, rising and falling instead of declining steadily into deeper water. Tunnels shrink and expand even as they change their shape, from roundish to oval to narrow slits."[1]

cool blue water and swimming down into a cave that wound underneath the island.

In theory, it's easy to understand the allure of underwater caves. They are shimmering blue jewels, worlds of silent airlessness, where scuba divers can float and drift as if freed from the bounds of gravity. It is also easy to understand why cave diving is dangerous. As Dr. Iliffe explained, "the big problem is that you have a ceiling over your head so you can't make a direct ascent to the surface. In the ocean if something goes wrong with your [scuba] gear you can swim to the surface. In a cave, you have a rock ceiling over your head and the only way you can get out is to swim back down the passageway that you came in."[2]

Not for the Faint of Heart

Gary Walten, an experienced cave diver, said there are three rules of cave diving: "One, don't kill yourself. Two, don't kill anyone else. Three, see rules one and two."[3]

While diving in caves, it's very easy to become disoriented. Swimming through water-filled tunnels deep underground can easily confuse divers to the point where they can't tell up from down. Further, a diver's fins can kick up silt and suddenly reduce visibility to zero. Divers have died only feet from a cave entrance that's become blocked by silt. Later, their bodies were found with fingers bloodied by the attempt to claw their way out through solid rock.

"That's why we don't promote cave diving," explained Bruce Ryan of the National Speleological Society. "If you don't realize all that can go wrong, cave diving isn't for you, because so much can go wrong."[4]

Basil Minns Blue Hole

Dr. Iliffe and Brian Kakuk hoisted their scuba gear out of the pickup truck and set off on a rugged ½-mile (0.8-kilometer) trail to the underwater cave known as Basil Minns Blue Hole. The Bahamas Islands are dotted with these blue holes. "When flying over them especially," Dr. Iliffe said, "they look like deep dark blue holes. Sometimes they're inland, in the jungles, or out in the ocean."[5] In fact, the holes are entrances to a wide-ranging and largely unexplored cave network that runs through a massive chunk of limestone with a surface area greater than 60,000 miles (100,000 kilometers).

During the limestone's 150-million-year existence, there were periods of extreme cold when water from the oceans froze into glaciers, causing the sea level to drop approximately 300 feet (90 meters). The limestone was exposed to air, allowing for cave tunnels to dissolve and spectacular stalagmites and stalactites to form. With the end of the last ice age about ten thousand years ago, the seas rose again, flooding the caves and leaving only relatively small bumps of rock—the Bahamas Islands—above water.

To enter Basil Minns Blue Hole, Iliffe and Kakuk waded out into a sapphire blue pond accompanied by an ever-present cloud of insects. They could see a submerged limestone ledge with a drop-off leading down to darker water. Beneath this ledge was the cave's slidelike entrance shaft. They strapped on four scuba tanks apiece, fit their regulators into their mouths, and slipped all the way into the warm water. Even though they were far from the ocean, the cave connected to the sea and tidal currents flushed in and out of the chambers, making it hard to swim. They kicked their fins cave style—from the ankle to avoid a "fin blast" that could stir up silt deposits. As they swam down the narrow shaft, their lamps illuminated the smooth limestone walls.

One cave diver has described the experience of plunging into a submerged cave in this way: "Imagine flying weightless through a blue palace, surrounded by glittering jeweled curtains

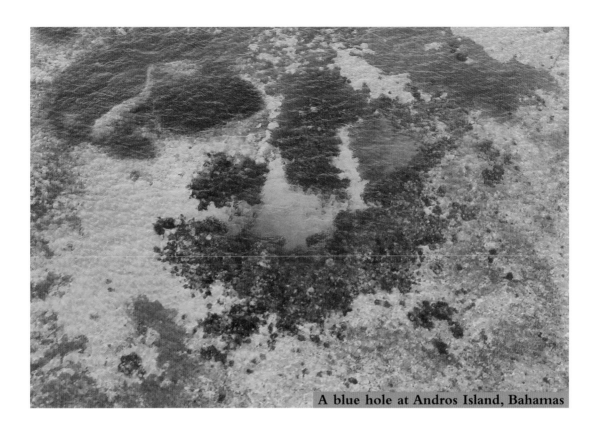
A blue hole at Andros Island, Bahamas

and columns. Streaks of distant daylight filter through the chamber from some place behind you. There are no sounds save the hiss of in-drawn breath and the gurgle of exhaled bubbles."[6]

As Iliffe and Kakuk swam down the shaft, they unrolled nylon guideline from a large spool. "We put plastic line arrow markers on the guideline and the arrow always points the direction out of the cave. . . ." Dr. Iliffe explained. "In case we get turned around, we can follow the line until we find an arrow. That way you don't get temporarily confused and think you're swimming out and really swimming farther into the cave."[7]

When the small dive computer attached to Dr. Iliffe's wrist indicated he was 1,000 feet (305 meters) into the cave, he stopped. He'd used up about one third of the air in his first tank, which is known as the stage bottle. The stage bottle is basically a precautionary air tank that the diver leaves en route in case he runs into trouble.

He snapped the stage bottle onto the guideline and began breathing from one of his two primary tanks. Giving a gentle kick with his fins, he continued swimming down the steep slot for another 1,000 feet (305 meters) or so until the cave tunnel started to rise upward, leading to a squeeze about the size of a mailbox. Dr. Iliffe was 150 to 160 feet (46 to 49 meters) beneath the Earth's surface.

Dr. Iliffe couldn't fit through a narrow opening with his tanks. He removed them and shoved them through the narrow opening while keeping the regulator in his mouth so he could breathe. He squirmed after them and found himself in a large air-filled cavern. "This room had some very beautiful stalactites and stalagmites. . . ." he said. "Their presence in the caves means that these caves must have been dry for considerable periods of time. . . . Eighteen thousand years ago, you could have walked into that cave instead of swum into it. And the stalactite and stalagmites in there are from that period and earlier."[8]

A sense of quiet awe filled him. He reflected on how "there's only been 3 or 4 people who have been into this cave or into this room and that's one of the unique thrills of cave diving. There's few places where you can do original exploration where you can be one of the first people in the history of the world to see some of these sights. It's a pretty unique experience. . . . Virtually all of the highest mountains in the world have been climbed and every place on the surface of the earth has been explored. It's only under the surface of the earth that discoveries still await."[9]

In the center of the room loomed a rock pile where sections of the ceiling had collapsed. He could not take off his regulator because the space was filled with hydrogen sulfide. The dissolved gas penetrated 70 feet (21 meters) deep into the water, making it appear smoky gray. "We can go into that [smoky layer] for only a limited amount of time," he said, "because it can be absorbed through the skin. It looks like a dust or a smoke cloud layer in the water."[10] Diving below this level, he saw crystal-clear water and a variety of animals swimming around.

"The rest of the cave has fairly strong tidal currents and so water is flushing in and out of the sea, but this one room is fairly far away and so water doesn't flush in and out, it's more stable," he explained.[11]

Dr. Iliffe removed vials from a pouch attached to his waist and very carefully approached a shrimplike creature. He waited for it to swim into his bottle, and then he put on the cap. "We want to get the animals out alive and in as good shape as we possibly can," he said. "We collect one animal per bottle. There's some fish we've seen in the cave that are up to 6 inches [15 centimeters] long. Most of the cave adapted animals are totally eyeless and typically have no body pigmentation."[12]

Dr. Iliffe and Brian Kakuk spent fifteen blissful minutes swimming around the cavern chasing after animals, some of which proved elusive. The divers were disappointed when their dive computers alerted them that their air was down to a point that would require them to turn around and head back. They followed the guideline back through the squeeze and up the slope to the stage bottles. Dr. Iliffe picked up his stage bottle and breathed from it until he was near the cave entrance, where he began the slow process of decompressing. During deep dives, nitrogen gas enters the bloodstream. In order to allow it to escape, divers need to ascend slowly. If they don't, the nitrogen bubbles in their bloodstream can cause paralysis or even death. Dr. Iliffe paused at depths of 40, 30, 20, and 10 feet (12, 9, 6, 3 meters), allowing his body to recover over a period of two hours before he climbed out of the water.

Back at the lab, he immediately transferred the creatures he'd collected into petri dishes and studied them under a microscope. Some of his cave animals swam too fast for him to photograph,

Dr. Iliffe took photos of the creatures collected at Basil Minns while they were still alive in order to record their natural state. As soon as a creature dies, its body contorts in unnatural ways.

so he put those petri dishes into a refrigerator to slow the animals down. After photographing the cave creatures, he preserved them in alcohol. Later, he would send the photos to experts all over the world who would help him determine if the creatures he'd found were related to known species, or entirely new animals never before seen.

"Everybody always asks me what are the practical aspects [of what I do], where are we going to make money on this, like that's the only thing that's worthwhile," Dr. Iliffe said with a rueful laugh. "Fortunately we have something."[13] One of his colleagues, Mark Slattery, has been researching sponges Dr. Iliffe retrieved from Bahamian caves. Dr. Slattery found that extracts from these sponges have potential anticancer and antimicrobial properties. This potential increases with sponges collected deeper into the cave. "Someday somebody's going to find a cure for cancer," Dr. Iliffe said. "Now where that's going to come from, I don't think anybody's got a clue. But who knows, it could come from very strange places like underwater caves."[14]

What pulls him underground is just old-fashioned curiosity. "What I do is basic science rather than applied research," he said. "Most of the work I do is trying to understand natural systems, see how they work, and what organisms make up the ecosystem."[15]

So far, his dives in the Bahamas have shown that animals living in caves on different islands are closely related despite the fact that they're separated by expanses of deep ocean. How could this be possible? Dr. Iliffe has three theories:

❏ The animals all share one ancestor who invaded different caves and whose offspring have since evolved in similar ways in a number of different caves.

❏ The animals may be able to swim at much greater depths than previously thought, in which case they'd be able to reach caves on other islands by either swimming through the deep oceans or by traveling through undiscovered deep cave passages beneath the seafloor.

❏ These creatures are the offspring of ancient animals that lived 100 million years ago. Back then, the continents were a single landmass. When the landmass broke up, the cave animals were spread farther apart.

Dr. Iliffe suspects that the third explanation is the most likely. This would mean that the cave creatures he collected in Basil Minns Blue Hole have been in existence since the time of the dinosaurs. "We can't go back and look at dinosaurs, but caves are like time machines," he said, his voice softening with reverence. "We can look at creatures who lived with dinosaurs but now only exist in these caves. Caves are like portals to lost worlds."[16]

CHAPTER NINE

Become a Cave Scientist!

Many of today's leading cave researchers started out as recreational cavers. Others were lured underground, almost against their will. Dr. Boston recalled that her first caving trip was into Lechuguilla: "It was the most grueling trip of my life (five days, 1,000 feet below the surface) and my only redeeming thought was that, should I live, I would never have to go back again. Of course, later, on the surface when my bruises were healing and the memory of my extreme discomfort and fatigue was fading, I realized that [the scientific possibilities meant] I had to go back. First, I had to learn to cave without killing myself."[1]

To pursue a career in cave science, you'll first need to get a bachelor of science degree in either cave science or a related field, such as geology or biology. To do your own research, you will need to get at least a master of science degree, and preferably a doctoral (Ph.D.) degree.

First, however, you'll want to go caving and see if it's the right activity for you. The National Speleological Society (NSS) oversees caving clubs, called grottoes, across the country. With a grotto, you can receive training and go on guided explorations of caves in your area. You can contact them by e-mail, at nss@caves.org, or by writing to 2813 Cave Avenue, Huntsville, AL 35810-4413, or by calling (256) 852-1300.

The only way to learn how to cave is to go with people who know what they're doing. As one caver explained, "Even if you are an experienced climber or hiker, your guides will (or should)

A student grotto of the Wittenberg University Speleological Society right before a cave-mapping expedition

Students sometimes get more adventure than they expected when going on a caving expedition.

spend a great deal of time talking to you about safety and conservation before they take you underground. They will want to see a certain determination and self-reliance in your thinking, to be sure that you won't get weird in a tight spot. . . . Even after you join a grotto, it may take a year or more before you are taken to any of the group's biggest or best caves (often kept secret). Be patient. Every caver I know who has taken the time to learn with an experienced group has made friends for life and has found a truly life-changing way of looking at the world."[2]

Source Notes

Introduction

1. Annette Summers Engel, personal interview, October 1, 2002.
2. Engel.
3. Engel.

Chapter One: A New Science

1. Michael Ray Taylor, Caves: Exploring Hidden Realms (Washington, D.C.: National Geographic, 2001), p. 7.
2. Evan Hadingham, "Subterranean Surprises." [Online] Available at http://www.smithsonianmag.si.edu/smithsonian/issues02/oct02/pdf/smithsonian_october_2002_subterranean_surprises.pdf, March 6, 2003.
3. Michael Ray Taylor, Cave Passages: Roaming the Underground Wilderness (New York: Scribner's, 1996), p. 108.
4. Feride Serefiddin, in written correspondence with author, October 2, 2002.

Chapter Two: The Power of Water

1. Mark Twain, "The Adventures of Tom Sawyer: Chapter XXIX." [Online] Available at http://www-2.cs.cmu.edu/People/rgs/sawyr-XXIX.html, March 6, 2003.

Chapter Three: Mystery at Carlsbad Caverns

1. Harvey R. DuChene and Carol A. Hill, "Introduction to the Caves of the Guadalupe Mountains Symposium," Journal of Cave and Karst Studies, August 2000, p. 53.
2. DuChene and Hill, p. 53.
3. Evan Hadingham, "Subterranean Surprises." [Online] Available at http://www.smithsonianmag.si.edu/smithsonian/issues02/oct02/pdf/smithsonian_october_2002_subterranean_surprises.pdf, March 6, 2003.
4. Jim White, "Jim White's Own Story." [Online] Available at

www.pbs.org/weekendexplorer/newmexico/carlsbad/carlsbad_white.htm,
November 18, 2002.

5. Donald Dale Jackson, Planet Earth: Underground Worlds (Alexandria, VA:
Time-Life Books, 1982), p. 89.

6. Richard Benke, "New Mexico Scientists Find Microbe Bites Helped Carve
Caves," The Associated Press, October 10, 2002.

7. Hadingham.

8. Sarah Holt, producer, Nova: The Mysterious Life of Caves (Boston: WGBH,
2002).

9. Holt.

10. Holt.

11. Benke.

Chapter Four: The Creepy Cave

1. Louise D. Hose, "Cave of the Sulfur Eaters." [Online] Available at
http://www.findarticles.com/cf_0/m1134/3_108/54343077/p1/article.jhtml?
term=%22Cave+of+the+Sulfur+Eaters, November 16, 2002.

2. Hose.

3. Peter Lane Taylor, Science at the Extreme: Scientists on the Cutting Edge of
Discovery (New York: McGraw-Hill, 2001), p. 45.

4. Taylor, p. 38.

5. Penelope Boston, "Exploring Acidworld." [Online] Available at
http://stage.agiweb.org/geotimes/aug00/acidworld.html, September 26, 2002.

6. Sarah Holt, producer, Nova: The Mysterious Life of Caves (Boston: WGBH,
2002).

7. Taylor, p. 39.

Chapter Five: Extremophiles

1. Steven Schultz, "Two Miles Underground." [Online] Available at http://www.
princeton.edu/pr/pwb/99/1213/microbe.shtml, November 2, 2002.

2. Sarah Holt, producer, Nova: The Mysterious Life of Caves (Boston: WGBH,
2002).

3. Jon Krakauer, "Descent to Mars." [Online] Available at www.airspacemag.com/
asm/Mag/Index/1995/ON/dtom.html, September 26, 2002.

4. Michael Ray Taylor, Dark Life: Martian Nanobacteria, Rock-Eating Cave Bugs,

and Other Extreme Organisms of Inner Earth and Outer Space (New York: Scribner's, 1999), p. 69.

5. Krakauer.

6. Peter Nelson, "The Cave That Holds Clues to Life on Mars," National Wildlife, August–September 1996, p. 41.

7. Taylor, p. 65.

8. Nelson, p. 42.

Chapter Six: Bears and Bats and Troglobites, Oh My!

1. "Underground, Overground," Geographical, October 2000, p. 98.

2. Richard Borowsky, personal interview, November 29, 2002.

3. Borowsky.

4. Borowsky.

Chapter Seven: Nature's Storm Drains

1. "Hot Jobs: Cave Geologist." [Online] Available at http://www.findarticles.com/ cf_0/m1590/12_55/55183100/p1/ article.jhtml?term=Hot+jobs+cave+hunter, November 20, 2002.

2. Jennifer Batz, "The Clan of the Cave Snail," Riverfront Times, March 6, 2002. Available at http://www.riverfronttimes.com/issues/2002-03-06/ feature.html/1/index.html

3. Batz.

4. Batz.

5. "Tumbling Creek Cavesnail Listed As Endangered." [Online] Available at http://midwest.fws.gov/Endangered/Snails/tcca-8-02-nr.html, November 22, 2002.

6. Denise Henderson Vaughn, "Karst in the Watershed." [Online] Available at http://www.watersheds.org/blue/earth/karst1.htm, November 18, 2002.

7. Vaughn.

8. Vaughn.

Chapter Eight: Cave Diving

1. Michael Agar, "The Yucatan's Flooded Basement," Smithsonian, April 1998, p. 96.

2. Tom Iliffe, personal interview, August 24, 2002.

3. Agar, p. 94.

4. Michael Ray Taylor, Cave Passages: Roaming the Underground Wilderness (New York: Scribner's, 1996), p. 21.

5. Todd Ackerman, "Unexplored Worlds: Cave Diver Tom Iliffe Goes Where No One has Gone Before." [Online] Available at http://www.tamug.tamu.edu/cavebiology/TexasMagazine.html, August 8, 2002.

6. Michael Ray Taylor, Caves: Exploring Hidden Realms (Washington, D.C.: National Geographic, 2001), p. 118.

7. Iliffe.

8. Iliffe.

9. Iliffe.

10. Iliffe.

11. Iliffe.

12. Iliffe.

13. Iliffe.

14. Iliffe.

15. Iliffe.

16. Iliffe.

Chapter Nine: Become a Cave Scientist!

1. Penelope Boston, "Life Below and Life Out There." [Online] Available at http://stage.agiweb.org/geotimes/aug00/lechuguilla.html, November 18, 2002.

2. Michael Ray Taylor, Cave Passages: Roaming the Underground Wilderness (New York: Scribner's, 1996), p. 274.

Further Reading

Books

Aulenbach, Nancy Holler, and Hazel A. Barton. Exploring Caves: Journeys into the Earth. Washington, DC: National Geographic, 2001.

Borden, James D., and Roger W. Brucker. Beyond Mammoth Cave: A Tale of Obsession in the World's Longest Cave. Carbondale, IL: Southern Illinois University Press, 2000.

Brock, M. Fenton. Bats. New York: Checkmark Books, 2001.

Burgess, Robert F. The Cave Divers. Locust Valley, NY: Aqua Quest Publishing, 1999.

Exley, Sheck. Caverns Measureless to Man. Trenton, NJ: Cave Books, 1994.

Stewart, P.K. Caving. Mechanicsburg, PA: Stackpole Books, 2002.

Stone, William, Barbara Am Ende, and Monte Paulsen. Beyond Deep: The Deadly Descent into the World's Most Treacherous Cave. New York: Warner Books, 2002.

Taylor, Michael Ray. Cave Passages: Roaming the Underground Wilderness. New York: Scribner's, 1996.

Taylor, Michael Ray. Caves: Exploring Hidden Realms. Washington, DC: National Geographic, 2001.

Taylor, Michael Ray. Dark Life: Martian Nanobacteria, Rock-Eating Cave Bugs, and Other Extreme Organisms of Inner Earth and Outer Space. New York: Scribner's, 1999.

Tuttle, Merlin D. America's Neighborhood Bats: Understanding and Learning to Live in Harmony with Them. Austin, TX: University of Texas Press, 1997.

Video

Ends of the Earth: The Secret Abyss of Movile Cave. New York: Unapix, 1997.

Journey into Amazing Caves. Laguna Beach, CA: MacGillivray and Freeman, 2000.

Nova: The Mysterious Life of Caves. Boston: WGBH, 2002.

Web Sites

Anchialine Caves and Cave Animals (Dr. Thomas Iliffe): www.cavebiology.com/

Bahama Caves Research Foundation:
    www.bahamacaves.com/pages/686289/index.htm

The Biology of Caves, Karst, and Groundwater:
    www.utexas.edu/depts/tnhc/.www/biospeleology/

The Cave Diving Web site: www.cavediving.com

Cavernet: Caving Mega-Links Page: www.caver.net/megalink.html

Deep Secrets: The Discovery and Exploration of Lechuguilla Cave:
    www.deep-secrets.com/index.html

Dr. Annette Summers Engel's homepage:
    www.geo.utexas.edu/chemhydro/Annette/ase_personal.htm

Dr. Diana Northup's homepage: www.i-pi.com/~diana/

Dr. Penelope Boston's homepage: www.ees.nmt.edu/boston/

Journey into Amazing Caves Web site: www.amazingcaves.com/f_home.html

Karst Geomicrobiology: The Active and Accessible Subsurface:
    www.geo.utexas.edu/chemhydro/Annette/karstgeo.htm

Life in Extreme Environments: www.astrobiology.com/extreme.html#dark

The Mars Society: Mars Desert Research Station:
    www.marssociety.org/MDRS/index.asp

The Movile Cave Project: The Cave That Time Forgot:
    www.geocities.com/RainForest/Vines/5771/

National Cave and Karst Research Institute: www.aqd.nps.gov/nckri/

National Caves Association: cavern.com/

National Park Service Cave and Karst Program:
    www.aqd.nps.gov/grd/geology/caves/

The National Speleological Society: www.caves.org/

Subsurface Life in Mineral Environments (SLIME):
    www.i-pi.com/~diana/slime/index.html

Take a Virtual Tour of the Deepest Cave in the United States (Lechuguilla):
    www.extremescience.com/LechuguillaCave.htm

The U. S. Caves Directory: www.goodearthgraphics.com/showcave.html

The Virtual Cave: www.goodearthgraphics.com/virtcave.html

Index

Page numbers in *italics* refer to illustrations.

DATE DUE